YO-CXJ-106

Contents

Intro	1	Instant Box	22
Folding	2	Inside Out Boat	24
Ice Cream Cone	3	Boat with Sail	26
Baby Bird	4	Flapping Bird	27
Man in Cap	6	Poser	29
Butterfly	8	Elephant	33
Jet Plane	10	Bull	36
Guinea Pig	12	Rhino	40
Specter	13	Sunshine Picture Frame	42
Sea Monster	14	Hanging Ornament	44
White Tailed Duck	18	Hedgehog	46
Seal	20		

Introduction

Origami just means "folding paper." It's that simple. However, just folding paper can produce some pretty amazing results. All it takes is a little patience and practice.

All of the designs in this book are explained in a series of easy steps. The words tell you what you have to do. The pictures show you what the paper will look like when you've done it, or sometimes when the fold is partway through. The pictures and the words go together and you need to look at both. In particular, you need to look out for the words that tell you to turn the paper over. If you miss seeing these, the pictures just won't make sense, and your paper will become something else entirely.

The easiest designs are at the front of the book. The more challenging ones are at the back. If you are new to origami it's a good idea to start easy and work up. Origami is like swimming. Anyone can learn to do it, but jumping straight in the deep end is not always the best strategy.

As well as this book, this pack also contains some paper to fold with. Most of the paper is colored on one side and white on the other. You will however also find some dark blue sheets of paper that are the same color on each side. These sheets are for use in making the Hedgehog, which is the final model in this book.

1

HOW TO MAKE AND CREASE A FOLD

This page shows you how to make and crease a basic corner-to-corner fold. Most other folds, like edge-to-edge folds, are made in exactly the same way.

The only difference is in the bits that you have to line up with each other before you start to crease. Until you get really good at folding paper, you should always fold with your paper lying on a hard flat surface, like a table or a large book.

1 Place the corners together accurately and use one hand to hold them in place.

2 Start creasing the fold in the center, then work outward both ways.

3 Crease softly at first so that you can, if necessary, adjust the fold a little to make sure it is in the right place.

4 Once you are sure your crease is in the right place, use your fingernails to make it really sharp.

ICE CREAM CONE

This is a traditional origami design.

You will need one piece of pink paper.

Start with your paper white side up.

1 Fold your square not quite in half, like this.

2 Fold one of the thin corners not quite up to the top so that the result looks like this.

3 Turn the paper over and fold the other corner upward in the same way. The point at the bottom should be sharp.

4 Fold one edge of the cone inward as far as it will go.

5 Turn the paper over and make the same fold on the other side.

6 Your Ice Cream Cone is finished. If you need to, you can glue the front and back flaps in place. You can slide a small piece of brown paper in between the layers to add a stick of chocolate.

BABY BIRD

Designed by David Mitchell.

You will need one piece of light blue paper.

Start with your paper white side up.

1 Fold in half corner to corner in both directions to mark the center, then open out.

2 Fold one corner into the center.

3 Open out. Fold the opposite corner inward to where the crease made in step 2 crosses the diagonal.

4 Open out, then fold the same corner inward again to where the crease made in step 3 crosses the diagonal.

5 Open out, then remake fold 3.

6 Fold the tip of the front layer downward to create a small white triangular flap.

4

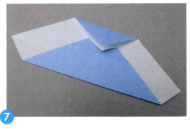

7

Fold the opposite corner downward to exactly cover this small flap so that the edges are aligned.

8

Fold the tip of this new top flap upward again to create a white square. This will become the beak.

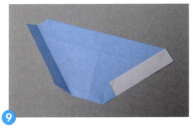

9

Turn over. Fold both sloping edges inward like this.

10

Fold both outside points inward in turn so that the corners of the white areas touch.

11

Fold both points outward again so that the inside edges of the flaps line up vertically.

12

Turn over. Open out the beak and adjust the angle of the wings so that your Baby Bird will stand on a flat surface. Feed it worms.

MAN IN A CAP

Designed by David Mitchell.

You will need one piece of red paper.

Start with your paper white side up.

1 Fold your square in half corner to corner both ways, then unfold.

2 Fold the top corner downward to the center.

3 Unfold, then use the crease you have just made to position this smaller downward fold.

4 Unfold, then use the crease you have just made to position this new upward fold.

5 Turn over. Fold the top point downward to where the creases made in steps 1 and 3 cross.

6 Fold the front flap downward along the existing crease.

6

7 Fold the top of the back layer downward as well, like this.

8 Fold the back layers downward over the front layers to form the face and cap.

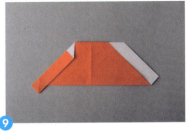

9 Turn over. Now fold both sloping edges inward to create the arms.

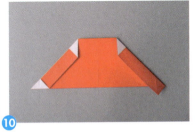

10 Fold the bottom corners of both arms upward to create hands.

11 Turn over. Fold both arms inward so that the tip of both hands rests on the upright center crease. They will spring open slightly, which is fine.

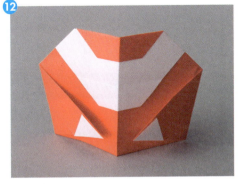

12 Fold the whole design backward slightly along the upright center crease. The Man in a Cap is finished. He will stand upright on a flat surface.

BUTTERFLY

Designed by David Mitchell.

You will need one piece of purple paper.

Start with your paper colored side up.

1

Fold in half edge to edge both ways then open out.

2

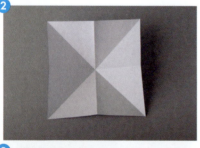

Turn over. Fold in half corner to corner both ways, then open out.

3

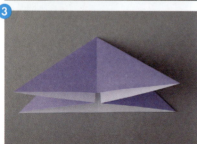

Bring the centers of all four edges together so that the paper collapses like this. All the creases you need have already been made.

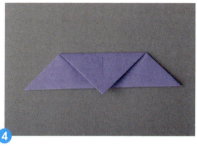

4 Fold the top point downward so that it ends up just below the bottom edge.

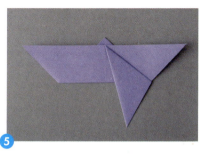

5 Turn over. Fold one wing downward like this.

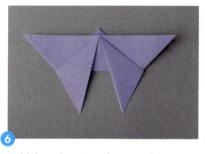

6 Fold the other wing downward to match.

7 Fold in half backward.

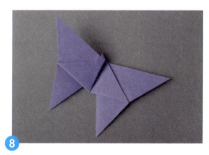

8 Fold the front wing downward to create the body

9 Repeat fold 8 on the other wing to complete your Butterfly. If you turn your butterfly over and lay it on a hard, flat surface you will be able to make the wings flap by gently pushing down on the head with one finger.

JET PLANE

Designed by David Mitchell.

You will need one piece of blue paper.

Start with your paper white side up.

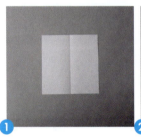

1 Fold in half edge to edge then open out.

2 Fold both the right and left hand edges onto the central crease.

3 Fold the top right corner across to the left.

4 Fold the top left corner across to the right.

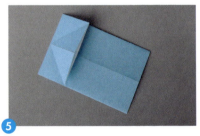

5 Turn over. Fold the top edge downward like this, using the diagonal creases as a guide.

6 Turn over. Collapse the top half of the paper like this, using the creases you made in steps 3, 4, and 5. (This is the same collapse that you made happen in step 3 of the Butterfly.)

7 Fold the front right hand flap out of the way then narrow the top point like this.

8 Do the same thing on the left-hand side then open out both front flaps again.

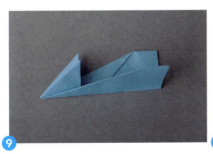

9 Fold in half like this.

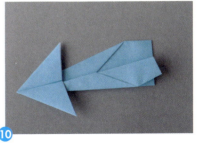

10 Fold the front flap in half downward to create the main wing. Fold the other flap downward as well to create an extra front wing.

11 Form the wings on the other side of the plane in the same way then separate the keel and the wings by lifting the wings upward at right angles (or perhaps just slightly more). The Jet Plane is ready to fly. Hold the keel at the balance point and launch with a gentle push.

GUINEA PIG

Designed by David Mitchell.

You will need one piece of brown paper.

Start with your paper white side up.

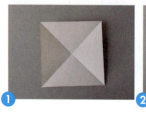

1 Fold in half corner to corner both ways then open out to mark the center of the paper.

2 Fold three of the corners into the center like this.

3 Turn over. Fold the fourth corner into the center as well to create a smaller square.

4 Fold two corners of this smaller square into the center, like this.

5 Two tiny folds are used to create the ears. Try to get both ears the same size and shape.

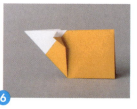

6 Fold in half so that the ears remain visible.

7 Fold both top corners inward like this.

8 Open out the folds made in step 7 then turn both corners inside out between the other layers. The creases you made in step 7 will help you do this.

9 Your Guinea Pig is finished.

SPECTER

This is a traditional origami design.

You will need one piece of black paper.

Start with your paper white side up.

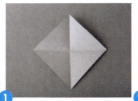

1. Fold in half corner to corner in both directions to mark the center of the paper then open out.

2. Fold all four corners into the center to create a smaller square.

3. Turn over. Fold all four corners of this smaller square into the center to create a smaller square still.

4. Turn over. Repeat Step 3

5. Turn over. Open out the center of three of the four flaps and squash them flat like this.

6. Lift up the fourth flap (without opening out its center), and then fold the design in half sideways. Crease firmly.

7. Open out and arrange the head and the sleeves in the way shown here. If you leave the body partly folded in half your Specter should stand on a flat surface.

SEA MONSTER

Designed by David Mitchell.

You will need one green piece of paper for the Sea Monster's head and at least five pieces of orange paper for the neck, spikes, and tail.

MAKING THE HEAD

Begin with a piece of green paper arranged white side up.

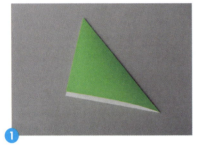

1 Fold the paper in half corner to corner.

2 Fold in half again like this.

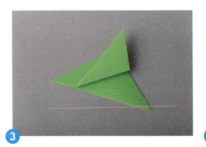

3 Create one of the Sea Monster's horns by folding the front layers upward like this.

4 Turn over. Create the second horn in the same way. The head is finished.

MAKING THE NECK

The neck is made by combining two pieces of paper. Begin with both pieces arranged white side up.

5 Fold the first square to step 2 of the head, then open out like this.

6 Fold the second square in half corner to corner, then open out.

7 Fold one edge onto the central crease.

8 Fold a second adjoining edge onto the central crease as well so that the edges meet.

9 Put the two pieces of the neck together like this. Piece one slides up inside piece two. The central creases of both pieces of paper line up.

10 Lock the two pieces together by folding the bottom point upward as far as it will go. Blunt the neck by folding the top point downward as shown. Fold in half sideways.

11 The head rests on top of the neck like this.

MAKING THE TAIL

12 Fold another piece of orange paper to step 2 of the head then fold the top layers outward to the right like this.

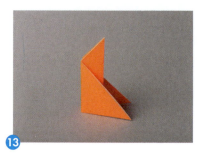

13 Turn over. Fold the other layers outward to match.

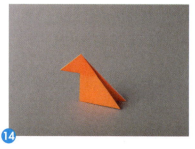

14 Fold the top point over the top of the other layers as far as it will go. Crease firmly.

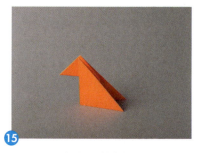

15 Open out the last fold then turn the top point inside out between the other layers. The tail is finished.

MAKING THE SPIKES

16

The humps are simply pieces of orange paper folded in half and then in half again in the way shown in steps 1 and 2 of *Making the head*. Your Sea Monster can have as many humps as you like.

COMBINING THE PIECES

Simply arrange your Sea Monster to look something like this.

17

WHITE-TAILED DUCK

This is a traditional origami design.

You will need one piece of yellow paper.

Start with your paper colored side up.

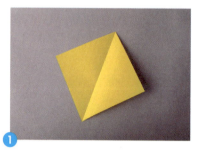

1 Fold in half corner to corner, then unfold.

2 Turn over. Fold two adjoining edges inward so that they meet on the diagonal crease you made in step 1.

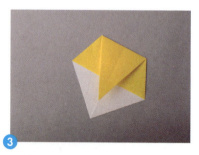

3 Fold the sharp point inward like this. It comes about two-thirds of the way into the white triangle.

4 Fold the front flap back on itself to form the head.

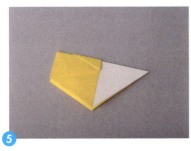

5 Fold in half along the crease made in step 1 so that the head remains visible.

6 Pull the neck upward like this and make a new crease so that it stays in position.

7 Pull the head upward and make a new crease so that it stays in position.

8 Fold both the bottom edges upward like this.

Tuck both the new flaps out of sight between the layers. Adjust the angle of the head if necessary. Your White-tailed Duck is finished.

9

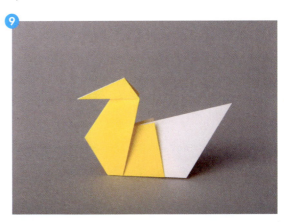

SEAL

This is a traditional origami design.

You will need one piece of blue paper.

Start with your paper white side up.

1

Fold in half corner to corner in both directions then open out.

2

Fold two adjoining edges inward so that they meet on one of the diagonal creases you made in step 1.

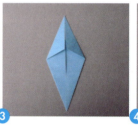

3

Fold the other two edges inward in a similar way.

4

Reach inside the front flaps, pull out the spare paper, and squash it to form two new pointed flaps like this.

5

Fold the tip of the top point downward. Also fold one of the triangular flaps in half upward to begin to form a front flipper.

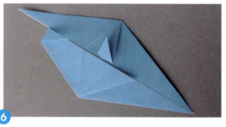

6

Form the back flippers by cutting the top flap in half upward with a pair of scissors. Fold the tip of the first front flipper across to the right.

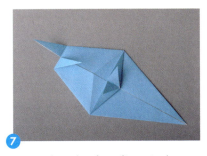

7

Create the other front flipper in the same way, then fold the design in half backward.

8

Lift the left hand point upward between the other layers to form the neck. Crease firmly.

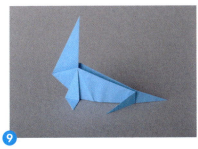

9

Fold the top point downward between the other layers to form the head.

10

Tuck the sharp point of the head back on itself in between the layers to blunt the nose.

Spread the front and back flippers so that your Seal will stand.

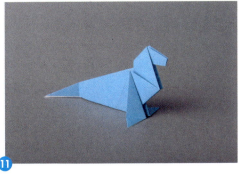

11

INSTANT BOX

This is a variation of a traditional origami design.

You will need one piece of blue paper.

Start with your paper white side up.

1 Fold in half edge to edge in both directions then open out.

2 Fold two opposite edges inward so that they meet in the center.

3 Unfold, then do the same thing with the other two edges.

4 Open out. You have divided your large square into sixteen smaller squares.

5 Fold two opposite edges inward so that eight of the small squares are folded in half.

6 Open out then remake the folds you made in step 3.

7 Fold both the edges in the center outward so that they line up with the outside edges.

8 Open out the folds you have just made. Fold all four corner squares in half inward.

9 Fold the other corners of both front flaps in half as well.

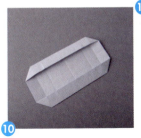

10 Fold both of the edges at the center outward using the creases made in step 7.

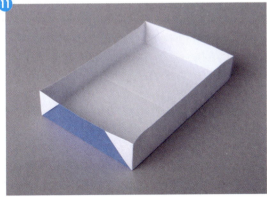

11

Now all you have to do is lift up the sides of the box and crease the corners to make them square.

Your Instant Box is complete.

1 Fold in half, edge to edge, then open out.

2 Fold both edges inward so that they meet in the center, then open out. You now have three upright creases dividing the paper into quarters.

24

3 Fold the right-hand edge onto the left hand crease.

4 Turn the left-hand edge of the front flap back on itself so that it lies along the right-hand crease.

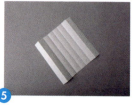

5 Open out completely. Repeat steps 3 and 4 in the other direction then open out completely again. Your paper will now be divided into eight thin strips like this.

6 Fold the paper in half backward, then fold three of the four corners inward like this.

7 Now fold the left hand half of the top layer across to the right like this.

8 Turn over. Repeat steps 6 and 7 on the other side of the paper.

9 Open up the center of the design and squash one end symmetrically like this.

10 Squash the other point symmetrically in the same way.

11 This is what the design should look like now.

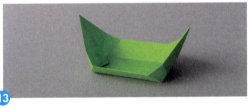

12 Turn over. Fold the top and bottom points inward in between the two upright creases. You need to do this as accurately as possible. Crease firmly.

13 Now turn the whole design inside out without letting either the bow or the stern come apart. The paper will become a bit crumpled in places as you do this, but you can smooth it out afterward. This picture shows what the boat looks like after it has been turned inside out.

14 Now fold both long sides inward so that they meet in the center. Crease firmly. You can smooth out any crumples at this stage.

15 Finally open out the sides again and shape the bow and the stern. The Inside-out Boat is finished. It floats well and can carry a small load.

BOAT WITH SAIL

You will need two pieces of paper, one green and one brown.

The green one becomes the boat and the brown one the sail.

To make the sail begin with your paper white side up.

1 Fold in half edge to edge.

2 Fold in half again like this.

3 Fold an Inside-out Boat to step 12 then fold in half so that it looks like picture 4. There is no need to crease this new fold. In fact, the paper may tear if you do, so just make it softly.

4 You will find the openings to two pockets along the top edge of the boat. Slide the two points of the sail into these pockets as far as they will go.

5 Open out the soft fold made in step 3 and crease the sail in both directions, forward and backward, so that it will stand.

6 Gently turn the boat inside out without damaging the sail, then shape the bow and the stern (see step 14 of the Inside-out Boat). Boat with Sail is finished.

FLAPPING BIRD

Designed by David Mitchell.

You will need one piece of orange paper.

Start with your paper white side up.

1 Fold in half corner to corner in both directions then open out.

2 Fold in half edge to edge in both directions then open out.

3 Turn over. Fold one corner inward so that the creases touch each other in the way shown here.

4 Fold one sloping edge of the top layer outward to lie along the folded upright edge.

5 Unfold. Fold the other sloping edge outward in the same way.

6 Fold the design in half backward. The bird's tail should pop up as you do this. Allow the paper to flatten into the shape shown here.

7 Fold the horizontal edge exactly onto the sloping crease below it. Note that this fold is made underneath the front layers of the tail.

8 Open out the last fold then turn the point inside out between the other layers to form a W of creases inside the body. This creates the head.

9 Fold the tip of the head downward to begin to form the beak.

10 Open out this last fold, then turn the beak inside out in between the layers of the head.

11 Pick the bird up by its head with your right hand. Take hold of the tip of the tail with your left hand and swing the tail downward so that the wings spread and flip upward.

12 Your Flapping Bird is finished. You can make the wings flap by holding the body in one hand and gently pulling on the tail with the other.

POSER

Designed by David Mitchell.

You will need two pieces of green paper.

MAKING THE BODY

Begin with the first piece arranged white side up.

1 Fold in half corner to corner.

2 Fold in half again then open out.

3 Fold both sharp corners onto the blunt one.

4 Open out the folds made in step 3. Fold the top corners downward so that the edges lie along the sloping creases made in step 3. The bits that look like the ears of a dog are actually Poser's feet.

5 Turn over. Fold the top layer of paper upward as far as it will go.

6 Fold the second layer upward as well so that the edges of the green triangle line up with the sloping edges of the feet.

MAKING THE HEAD

Fold the second piece of paper to step 3 of the body then turn it over.

7 Fold the top two layers upward like this.

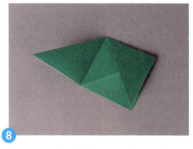

8 Open out the folds made in step 7, turn the paper over, then open out the left-hand point.

9 Fold the right hand corner inward and crease firmly. Use the crease made in step 7 to help you position this fold accurately.

10 Repeat step 9 on the other half of the paper.

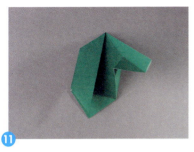

11 Open out the last two folds, then turn both points inside out in between the layers.

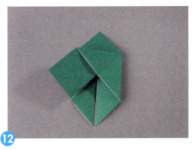

12 Turn over. Fold the top layer diagonally upward to the left.

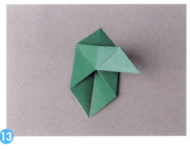

13 Fold the new flap across to the right and squash flat to form a point like this.

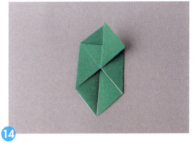

14 Fold the point of this flap upward. Crease firmly.

15 Undo fold 14. Swing the pointed flap across to the left and repeat step 14 in the opposite direction.

COMBINING THE PIECES

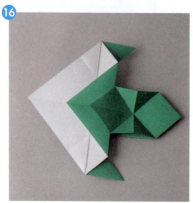

Open out folds 12 to 15, then slide the body inside the layers of the head like this.

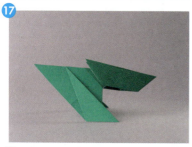

Fold in half downward. This will lock the body and the head together.

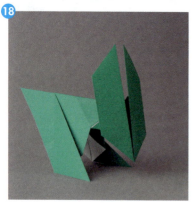

Stand Poser upright and he will balance on his feet. With a little experimenting you will find it possible to use the folds of Poser's neck to arrange his head in lots of different positions like this.

ELEPHANT

Designed by David Mitchell.

You will need two pieces of black paper.

MAKING THE BODY

Begin with one piece of paper arranged white side up.

1 Fold in half edge to edge both ways then open out.

2 Fold two opposite edges into the center, crease, then unfold.

3 Fold the same edges inward to lie along the creases you have just made.

4 Fold both new outside edges inward using the crease you made in step 2.

5 Fold in half backward so that the Elephant's legs are visible.

MAKING THE HEAD

Begin with the second square arranged white side up.

6 Fold in half corner to corner, then unfold.

7 Fold two adjoining edges onto the central crease so that the edges meet.

8 Fold in half.

COMBINING THE PIECES

9 Slide the legs inside the body like this. Look at how the bottom point of the body lines up with the front edge of the back legs. You can glue the two pieces together at this stage if you find it easier to do so, though this is not essential to the design.

10 Open out to this position, then fold the white triangle inward as far as it will go to lock the two pieces together.

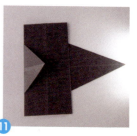

11 Turn over. Fold the point backward along the line of the body.

FORMING THE EARS AND TRUNK

12 Open out the long point (which will become the trunk and the ears) and fold in half again.

13 Form the ears by crimping the front point around the body. To do this, hold the body in one hand and the trunk in the other. Bring the trunk downward and allow the sides to spread outward along the line of the crease made in step 12. Squash to look like picture 14.

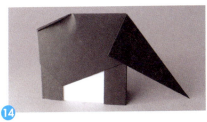

14 Make a fold to shape the back of the body, like this. Undo this fold and turn the point inside out in between the layers.

15 Make three small folds to shape the trunk.

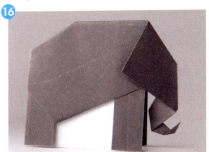

16 Open out all three folds. Remake the first two by turning them inside out in between the layers. Remake the third by turning it inside out outside the layers. Once you have done this your Elephant is finished.

BULL

Designed by David Mitchell.

You will need three pieces of orange paper.

MAKING THE BODY

Bull's body is made from two pieces of paper each of which is folded in exactly the same way. Begin with the paper arranged white side up.

1 Fold in half corner to corner in both directions to mark the center, then unfold.

2 Fold two opposite corners to the center.

3 Undo the last two fold,s then turn over. Fold the same corners inward to the point where the creases made in step 2 cross the diagonal crease.

4 Fold in half sideways so that the small white triangles remain visible.

5 Slide one piece inside the other like this.

6 Fold in half downward to lock the two pieces together then make a small fold to form the tail.

MAKING THE HEAD

7 Fold the third square in half, corner to corner, open it out and use scissors to cut along the diagonal to separate the two halves. Only one half is required.

8 Arrange the paper white side up then fold in half downward.

9 Open out. Fold both the sharp corners onto the blunt corner, like this.

10 Fold one of the lower sloping edges into the center to create a triangular flap.

11 Stand the flap upright, separate the layers, then squash it flat symmetrically. The white point this creates is one of the horns.

12 Fold the tip of the horn upward.

13 Open out the last fold then fold the entire horn upward along the line of the edge of the front layer of the paper.

14 Open out the last fold and repeat steps 10 through 13 on the other half of the paper.

15 Fold in half backward and arrange like picture 16.

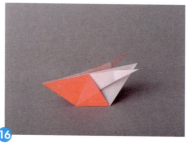

16 Fold the left hand point in half downward.

17 Fold the tip of the point inward again. Crease firmly.

18 Open out the last two folds, then turn the point inside out in between the layers using the creases made in step 16.

19 Lock the layers of the nose together by remaking fold 17 inside the layers.

COMBINING THE PIECES

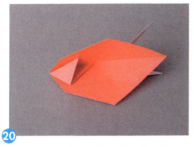

20 This is what the inside of the head should look like.

21

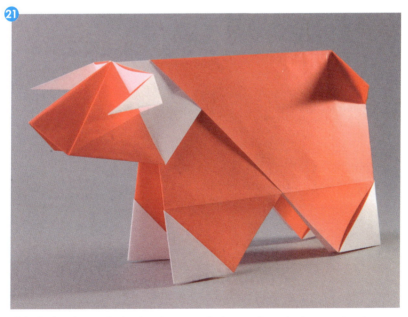

Slide the head onto the body in between the layers. Pose the horns using the existing creases. Your Bull is finished.

RHINO

Designed by David Mitchell.

You will need four pieces of blue paper.

MAKING THE BODY

The pieces you need to make the Rhino's body are exactly the same as the ones you used to make the body of the Bull (see steps 1 to 4), except that when you make the Rhino's back legs you need to fold two pieces of paper together at the same time. This is because you need extra weight at the back to balance the weight of the head. If you don't do this your Rhino will fall over forward and plow a furrow in the ground.

5 Slide the front legs inside the layers of the back legs so that the white triangles of the hooves are still just visible.

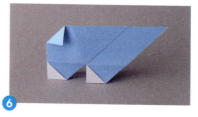

6 Fold in half downward, then make a small fold in the double layers of the back legs to create a tail. Crease firmly.

MAKING THE HEAD

Begin with steps 1 through 4 of the Seal.

7 Swing the bottom flap upward behind the top flap.

8 Fold the tip of the front flap inward to where the sloping creases meet.

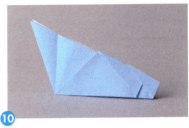

9

Now fold the tip of the back layer inward as well so that the paper looks like this. Fold in half backward and arrange like picture 10.

10

Lift both horns upward in turn and make new creases to hold them in place.

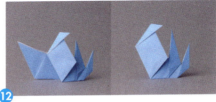

11

Fold one ear upward.

12

Fold the tip of the ear forward. Turn over and repeat the last two folds to create the other ear as well.

COMBINING THE PIECES

Stand the body upright and just place the head in position on the neck. Your Rhino is ready to charge.

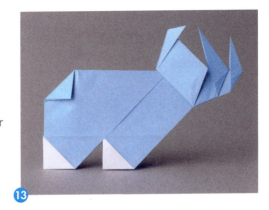

13

SUNSHINE PICTURE FRAME

Designed by David Mitchell.

You will need one piece of yellow paper.

Begin with the paper arranged white side up.

1 Fold in half corner to corner in both directions to mark the center, then open out.

2 Fold all four corners into the center.

3 Open out and turn over. Fold two opposite edges inward so that the edges meet in the center.

4 Open out then fold the other two corners inward in the same way.

5 Open out. Your paper should now look like a shallow bowl. At this stage you need to find a picture to frame and cut it to size so that it fits inside the central square.

6 The part of the picture you want to be able to see inside the frame must be right in the center.

42

7 Using the existing creases, bring the center of each edge into the center. The result will look like this.

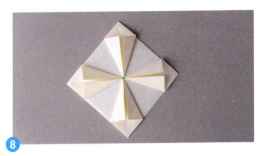

8 The front layer of the paper is divided into four separate squares. Fold the inside edges of each of these squares inward so that they meet on the diagonal creases. This will create eight small triangular flaps.

There are four sharply pointed flaps in the center. Fold these outward as far as they will go.

43

9 Stand each of these creases up in turn, separate the layers and squash them flat symmetrically. (This is the same move you used to create the Bull's ears.)

10

There are four more flaps in the center. Fold these outward as well to reveal your picture. The Sunshine Picture Frame is finished.

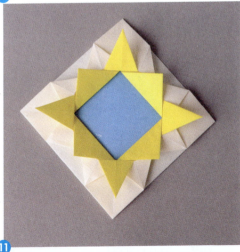

11

HANGING ORNAMENT

Variation on a traditional design.

You will need six pieces of green paper.

The Hanging Ornament is made from six identical units, or modules, which are joined together with glue.

Steps 1 to 9 of this design are the same as for the Sunshine Picture Frame, except that you don't need a picture and you begin with your paper arranged colored side up.

10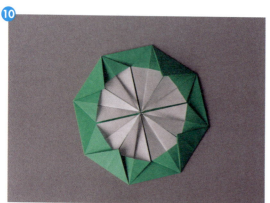

Fold all four corners inward using the points of the flaps you squashed flat in step 9 as a guide. Crease firmly. These flaps are used to join the six modules together.

11

Begin assembling the Hanging Ornament by gluing two modules together like this. Try not to get any glue on the outside of the modules. A glue stick will work well because it doesn't make the paper go stretchy.

12 Add a third module to form a corner.

13 Add the final three modules one by one to create a cube.

14

The Hanging Ornament is finished. You can hang the ornament using a small ball attached to a thread. The ball should be just small enough to be pushed through one of the holes, but too large to slip out again. You can make a suitable ball by crumpling another sheet of paper and attach the thread with a staple.

The Hedgehog is created by combining part of a spiny modular ball with a simple face. You will need one piece of orange paper for the face and five pieces of dark blue paper for the spines. The dark blue sheets you need are the ones that are the same color on both sides.

You need to begin by folding five pieces of paper to step 9 of the Sunshine Picture Frame, except that you don't need to worry about inserting a picture. Because the paper is the same color both sides you can begin with it either way up.

10

Take four of the modules and arrange them spines upward. Fold all four corners backward (you had to fold them forward when making the Hanging Ornament) using the points of the flaps you squashed flat in step 9 as a guide. Crease firmly.

11

Glue these modules together with the spines outside and the corner flaps inside (you left them outsides when making the Hanging Ornament) so that two adjacent faces of the cube are missing.

12

Arrange the fifth module spines upward as well. Fold three corners of this module inward in front in a similar way.

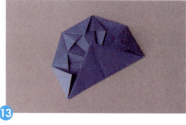

13

Fold the last corner inward as well, like this. Crease firmly. This large triangular flap is the base on which the Hedgehog will sit. Once you have creased it firmly open the flap most of the way out.

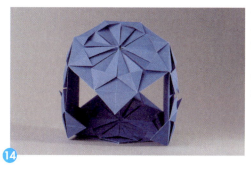

Glue this module onto the others using the small corner flaps. The spines on this module go on the inside not the outside. You will have a cube with one face missing.

MAKING THE FACE

Begin with the paper arranged white side up.

Fold in half edge to edge both ways, then unfold.

Fold two adjacent corners into the center.

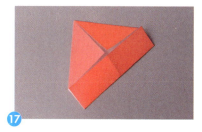

Fold the long edge into the center as well.

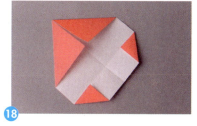

Open out the last fold. Fold the other two corners inward using the crease you just made as a guide.

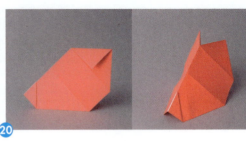

19 Turn over. Fold the tip of the long point inward to blunt the nose.

20 Fold in half backward then fold the top right hand corner inward using the crease made in step 3 as a guide, then turn inside out between the layers.

COMBINING THE PIECES

Stand the spines on the large triangular flap of the fifth module, spread the two sides of the face to make it three-dimensional, and slide the face inside the spines. Adjust the angle of the large flap the spines sit on and the angle of the small flaps that surround the face until it looks like this. Your Hedgehog is finished.

21
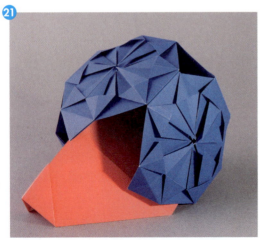